NICE & EASY
DOT-TO-DOT
PUZZLES

Conceptis Puzzles

PUZZLE
WRIGHT
PRESS

New York

PUZZLE
WRIGHT
PRESS
New York

An Imprint of Sterling Publishing
387 Park Avenue South
New York, NY 10016

ISBN 978-1-4549-1200-2

Distributed in Canada by Sterling Publishing
C/o Canadian Manda Group, 165 Dufferin Street
Toronto, Ontario, Canada M6K 3H6
Distributed in the United Kingdom by GMC Distribution Services
Castle Place, 166 High Street, Lewes, East Sussex, England BN7 1XU
Distributed in Australia by Capricorn Link (Australia) Pty. Ltd.
P.O. Box 704, Windsor, NSW 2756, Australia

For information about custom editions, special sales, and premium and corporate purchases,
please contact Sterling Special Sales at 800-805-5489 or specialsales@sterlingpublishing.com.

Manufactured in the United States of America

2 4 6 8 10 9 7 5 3

www.puzzlewright.com

•••••••••• Contents ••••••••••

•••••• Introduction ••••••

D o you like to connect dots and make amazing line art? If so, you've come to the right place! The 80 puzzles that follow will have you connecting thousands of dots and marveling at your own artistic skill. All you need is a pencil, a keen eye, a steady hand, and the ability to count. All set? Then let's get started!

If you've never solved a dot-to-dot puzzle before, here's how it works: find the number 1 somewhere on the page, then place your pencil on the dot next to it. Draw a straight line over to the dot next to the number 2, then draw another line to the dot next to the number 3, and so on. Eventually, you'll run out of dots and the picture will be complete (the final dot will always be a star). Feel free to hold it at arm's length and admire your handiwork!

Sometimes dots have been placed so they're overlapping, but that's okay; the dot with the lowest number will always be on top, and you'll see any future dots in that location peeking out from beneath the first dot. You may need to visually survey an area to determine which dot goes with which number, and remember that sometimes the next dot may be back the way you came from (or even along the same path you just created).

After you've completed each puzzle in pencil, you might want to go back over the correct path with a pen or colored pencil. You could even bust out the crayons and do some coloring! In any case, please enjoy the puzzles that follow and check out the other books in the Connectivity series. Visit us at www.conceptispuzzles.com for more ways to have fun and get smart.

—Conceptis Puzzles

ANSWER, PAGE 88

ANSWER, PAGE 89

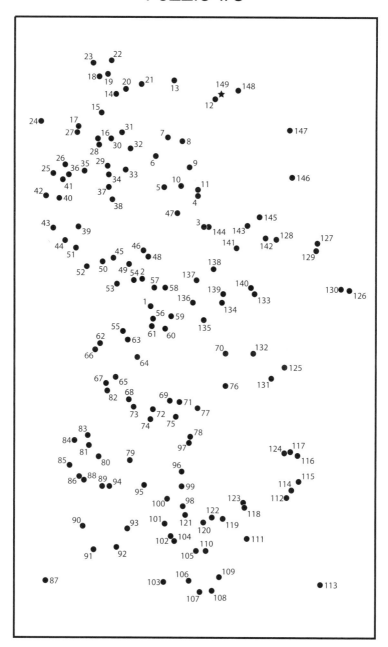

ANSWER, PAGE 90

•••••••••• Puzzle #6 •••••••••

ANSWER, PAGE 90

11

ANSWER, PAGE 91

ANSWER, PAGE 92

ANSWER, PAGE 93

ANSWER, PAGE 93

17

18

ANSWER, PAGE 95

ANSWER, PAGE 96

ANSWER, PAGE 97

ANSWER, PAGE 97

25

ANSWER, PAGE 99

ANSWER, PAGE 100

ANSWER, PAGE 101

ANSWER, PAGE 102

ANSWER, PAGE 102

ANSWER, PAGE 103

ANSWER, PAGE 103

ANSWER, PAGE 104

ANSWER, PAGE 105

ANSWER, PAGE 107

45

ANSWER, PAGE 111

ANSWER, PAGE 115

ANSWER, PAGE 116

63

ANSWER, PAGE 117

ANSWER, PAGE 118

ANSWER, PAGE 120

ANSWER, PAGE 122

ANSWER, PAGE 123

ANSWER, PAGE 124

ANSWER, PAGE 124

ANSWER, PAGE 125

ANSWER, PAGE 126

ANSWER, PAGE 126

ANSWER, PAGE 127

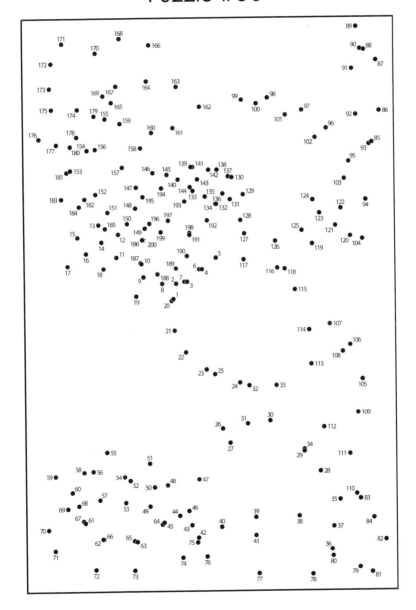

Answers

Puzzle #1

Puzzle #2

Puzzle #3

Puzzle #4

Puzzle #5

Puzzle #6

Puzzle #7

Puzzle #8

Puzzle #9

Puzzle #10

Puzzle #11

Puzzle #12

Puzzle #13

Puzzle #14

Puzzle #15

Puzzle #16

Puzzle #17

Puzzle #18

Puzzle #19

Puzzle #20

Puzzle #21

Puzzle #22

Puzzle #23

Puzzle #24

Puzzle #25

Puzzle #26

Puzzle #27

Puzzle #28

Puzzle #29

Puzzle #30

Puzzle #31

Puzzle #32

Puzzle #33

Puzzle #34

Puzzle #35

Puzzle #36

Puzzle #37

Puzzle #38

Puzzle #39

Puzzle #40

107

Puzzle #41

Puzzle #42

Puzzle #43

Puzzle #44

Puzzle #45

Puzzle #46

Puzzle #47

Puzzle #48

Puzzle #49

Puzzle #50

Puzzle #51

Puzzle #52

Puzzle #53

Puzzle #54

Puzzle #55

Puzzle #56

Puzzle #57

Puzzle #58

Puzzle #59

Puzzle #60

Puzzle #61

Puzzle #62

Puzzle #63

Puzzle #64

Puzzle #65

Puzzle #66

Puzzle #67

Puzzle #68

Puzzle #69

Puzzle #70

Puzzle #71

Puzzle #72

Puzzle #73

Puzzle #74

Puzzle #75

Puzzle #76

Puzzle #77

Puzzle #78

Puzzle #79

Puzzle #80

127